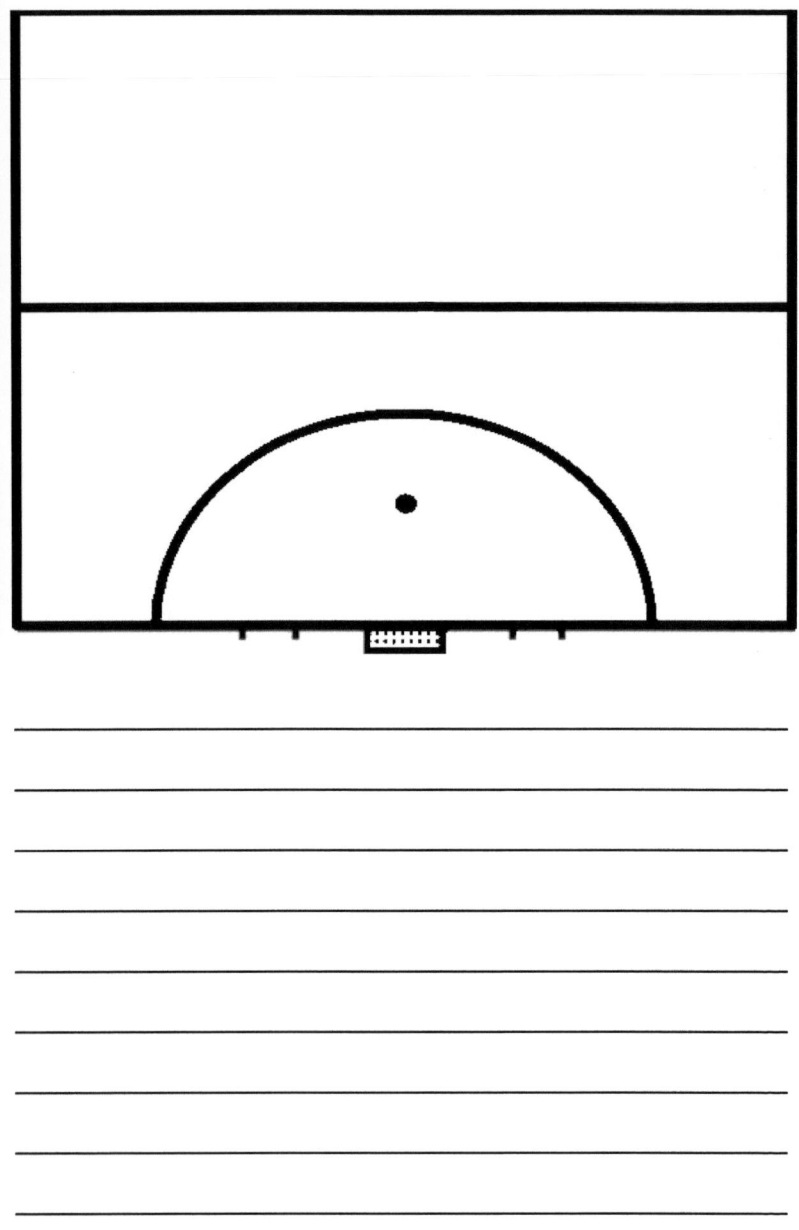

Theo von Taane

Field Hockey 2 in 1 Tacticboard & Training Workbook

The 2 in 1 Tacticboard & Training Workbook for fast creation of coaching instructions/game tactics and schemes, doesn't only offer sport specific preprints (playing field and space for notes), but also a cover, usable as a dry erase panel (whiteboard pen is needed).

ADVANTAGES:
- notebook with sport specific preprints (playing field) for fast and simple sketching of coaching instructions/game tactics and schemes

- If all pages of the notebook are used, the cover is still a dry erase panel (tacticboard)

- Due to a handy format, the notebook can be comfortably used in any situation (e.g. on the way or on the playing field)

- Perfect for spontaneous collection of ideas or as a memorization tool

- Practical handling due to easy pocket format

Bibliografische Information der Deutschen Nationalbibliothek:
Die Deutsche Nationalbibliothek verzeichnet diese Publikation in der Deutschen Nationalbibliografie; detaillierte bibliografische Daten sind im Internet über http://dnb.dnb.de abrufbar.

© 2016 Theo von Taane; 2. Auflage

Texte und Illustrationen: **Theo von Taane**

Herstellung und Verlag: BoD – Books on Demand, Norderstedt

ISBN: 9783734749810

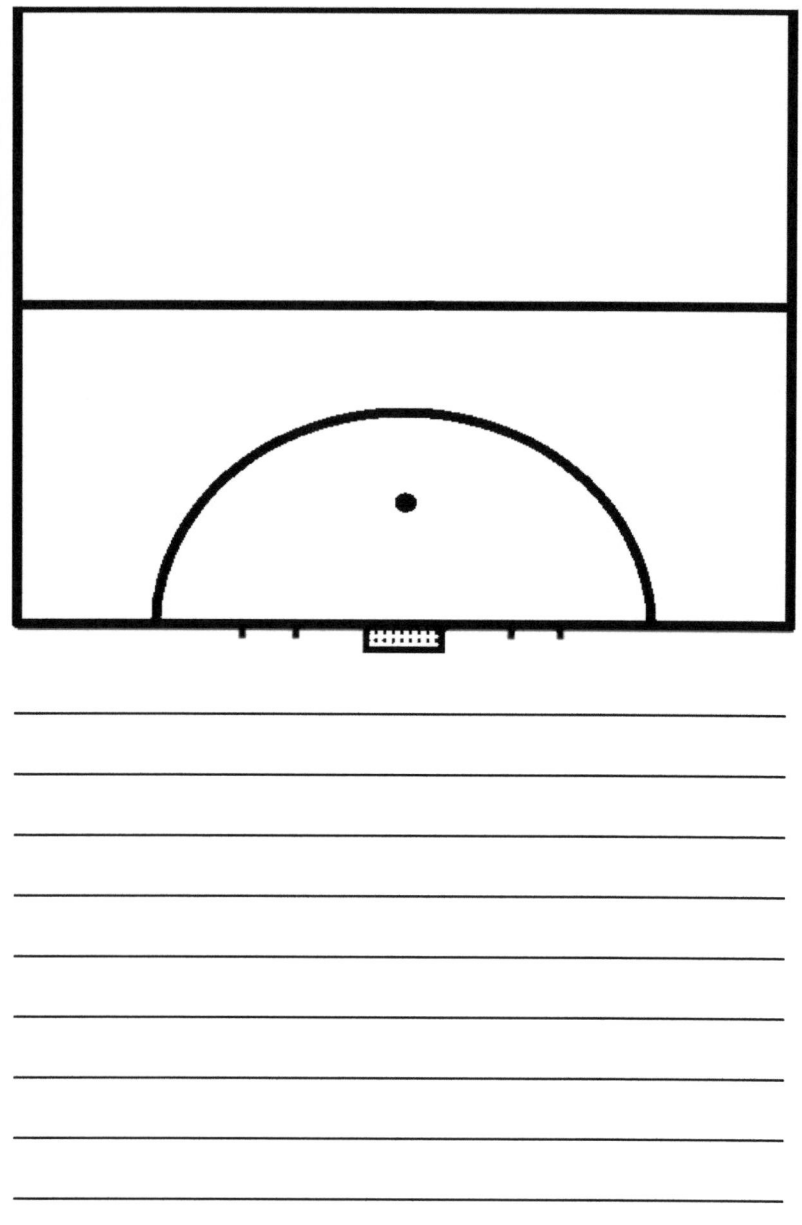

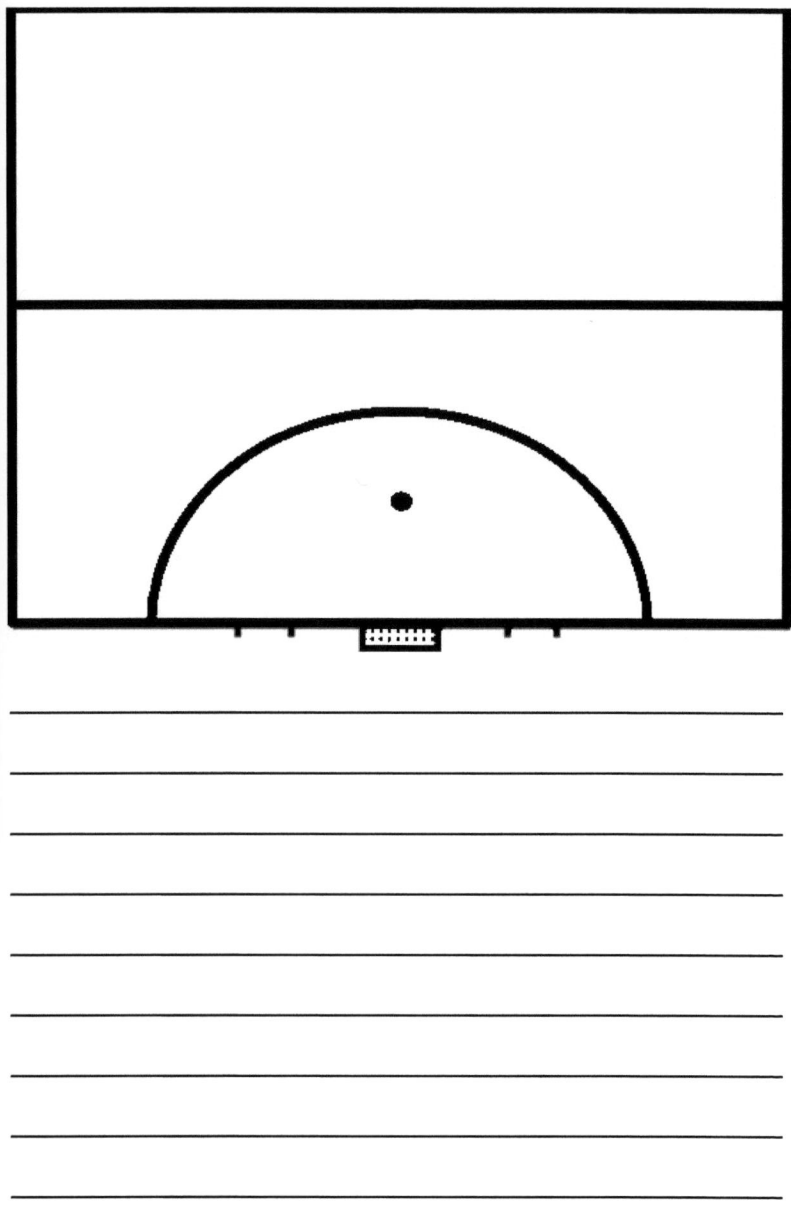

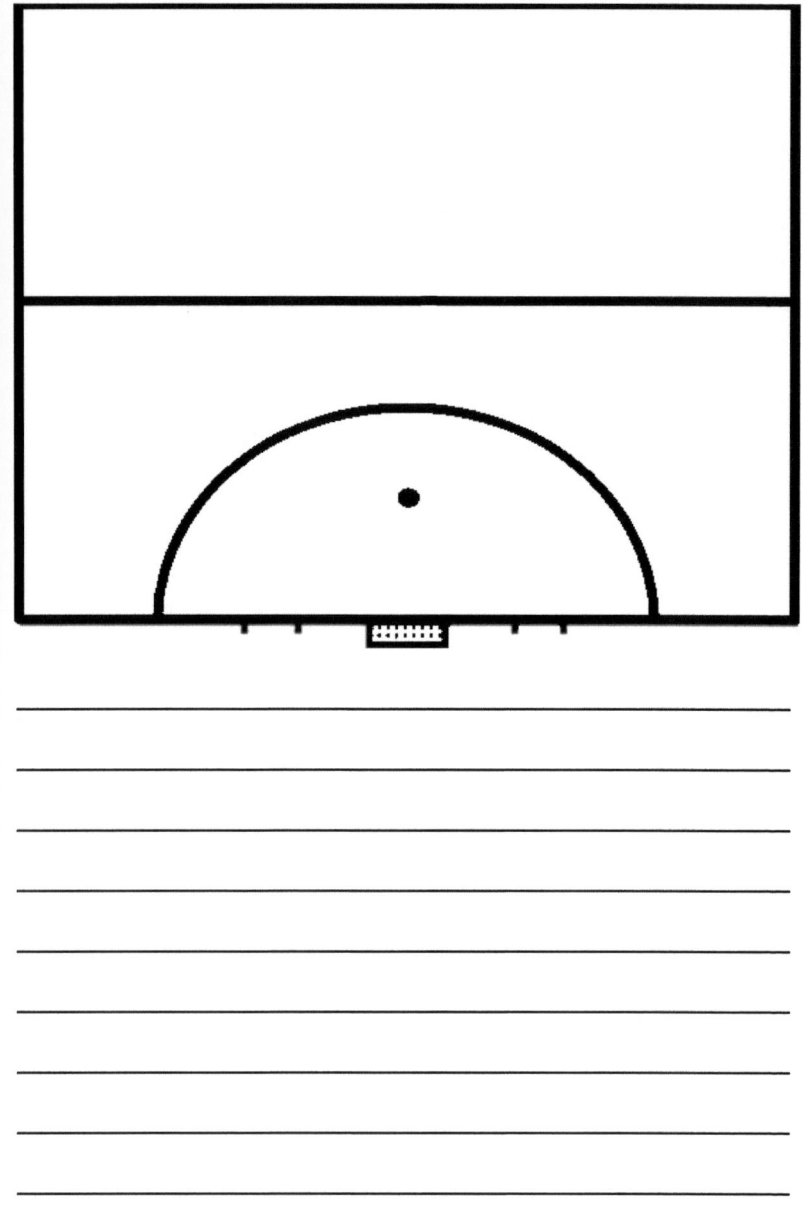

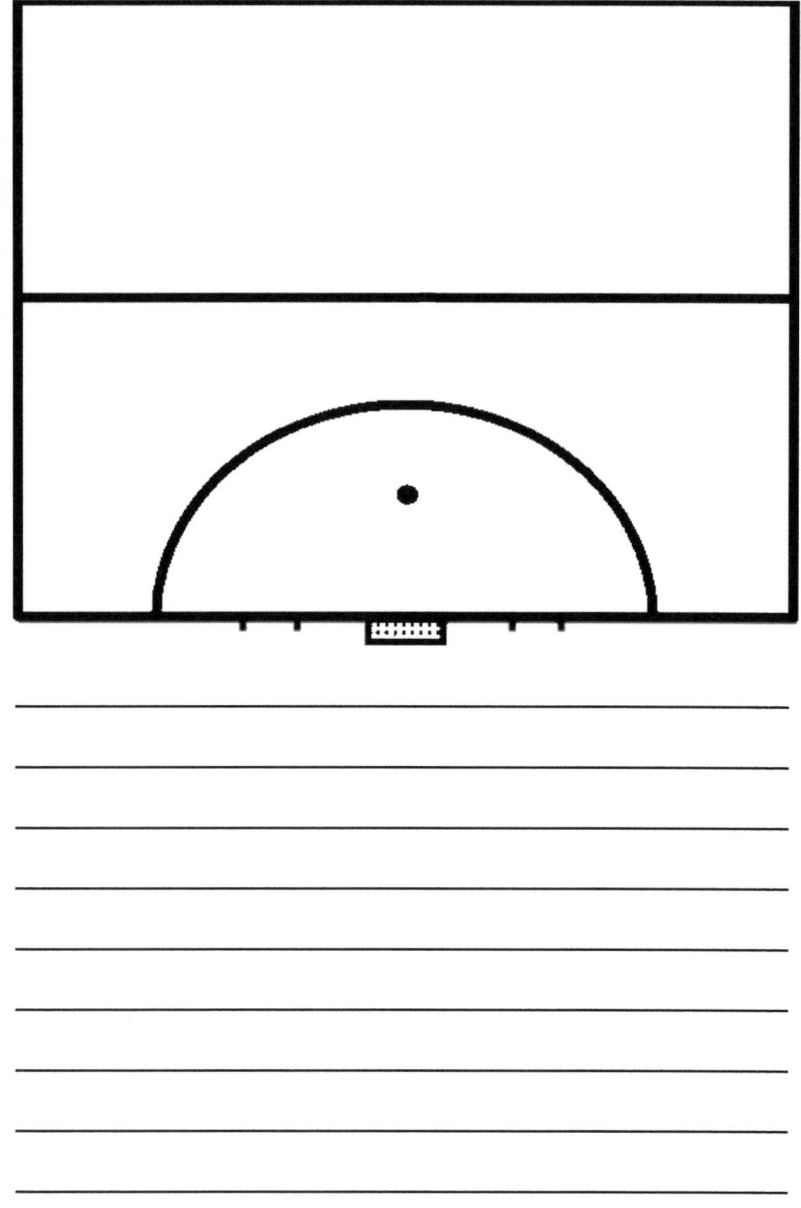

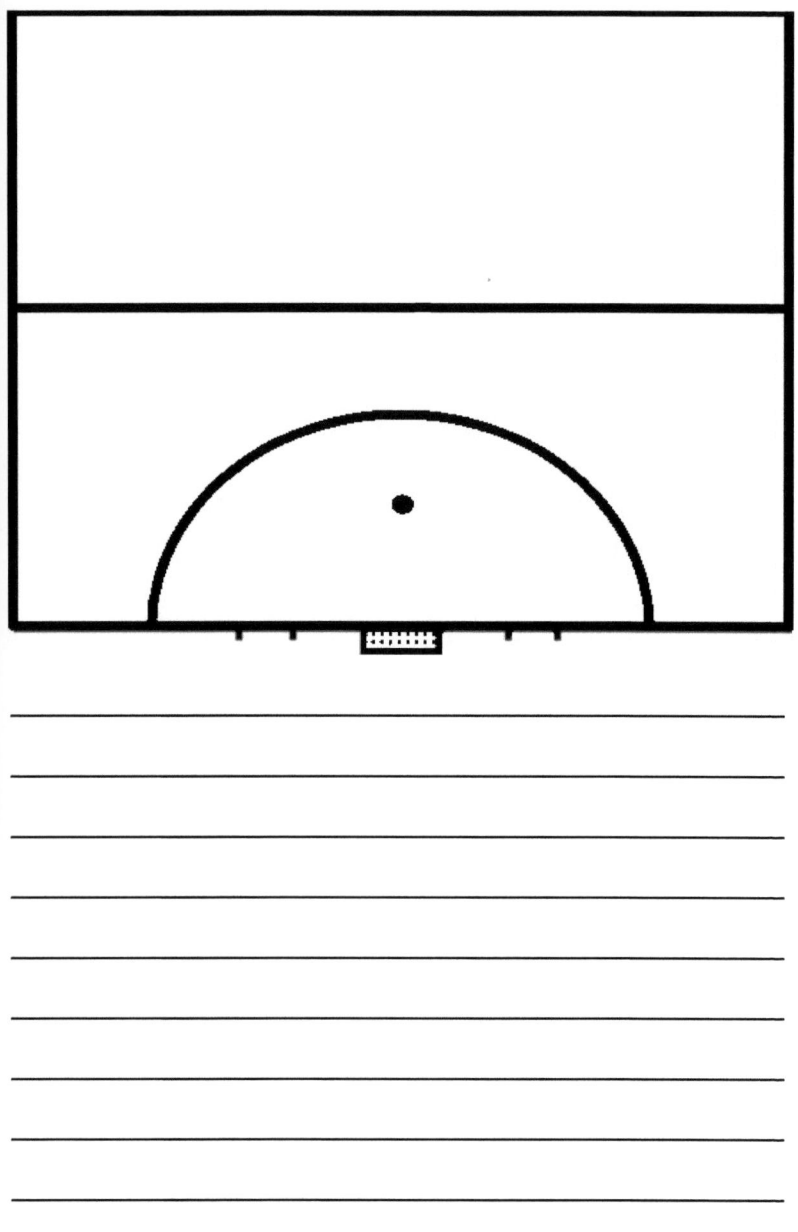

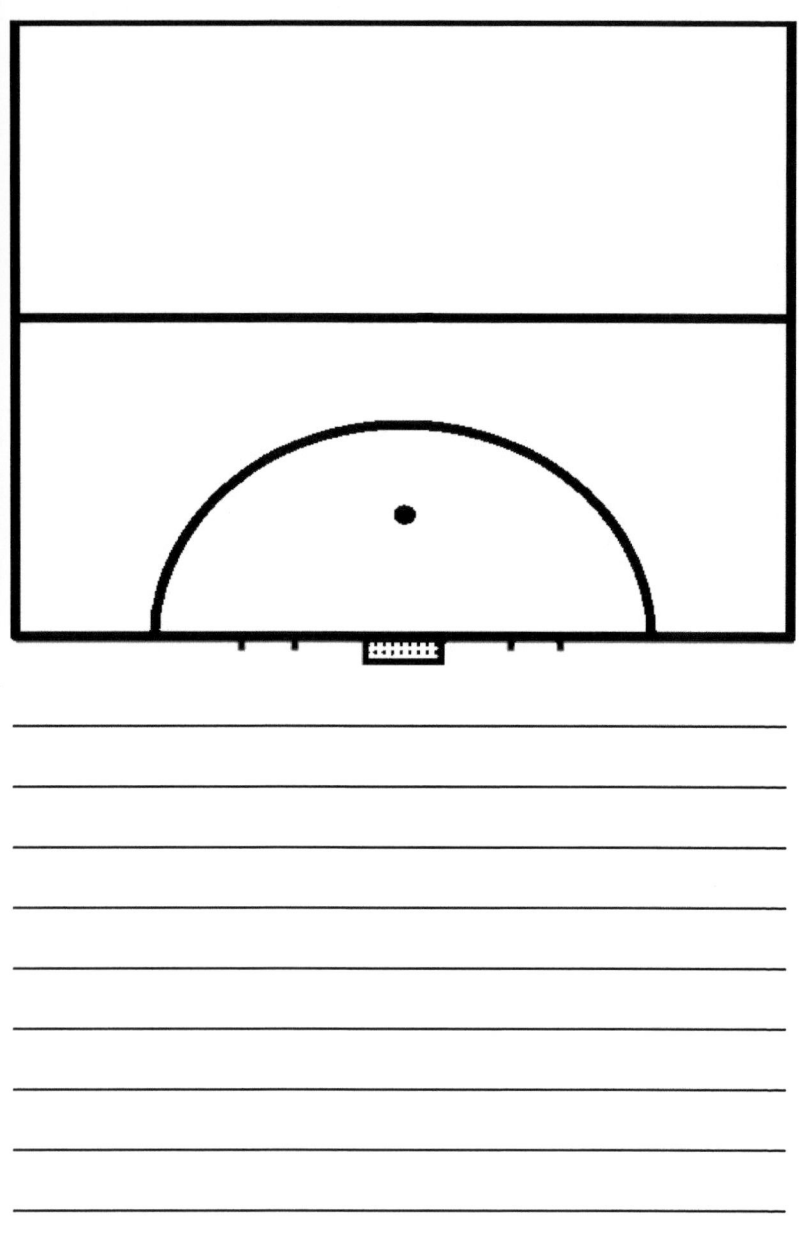

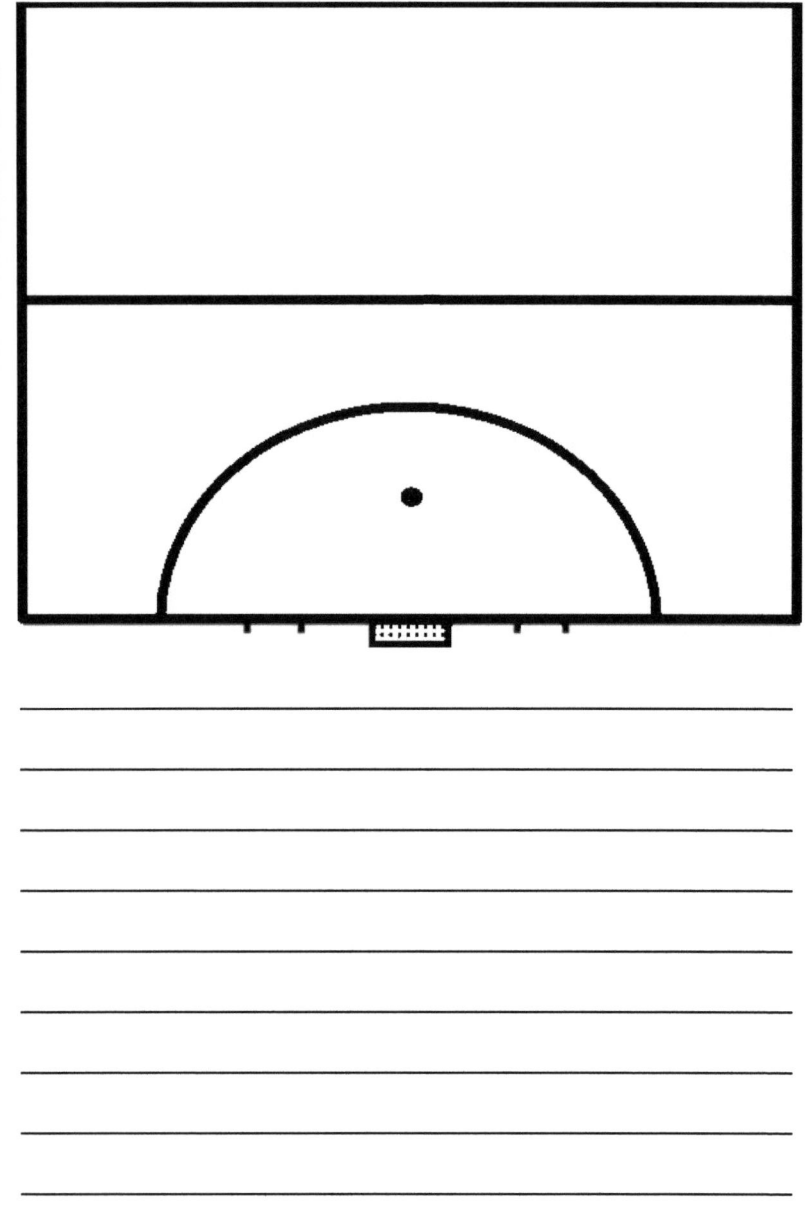

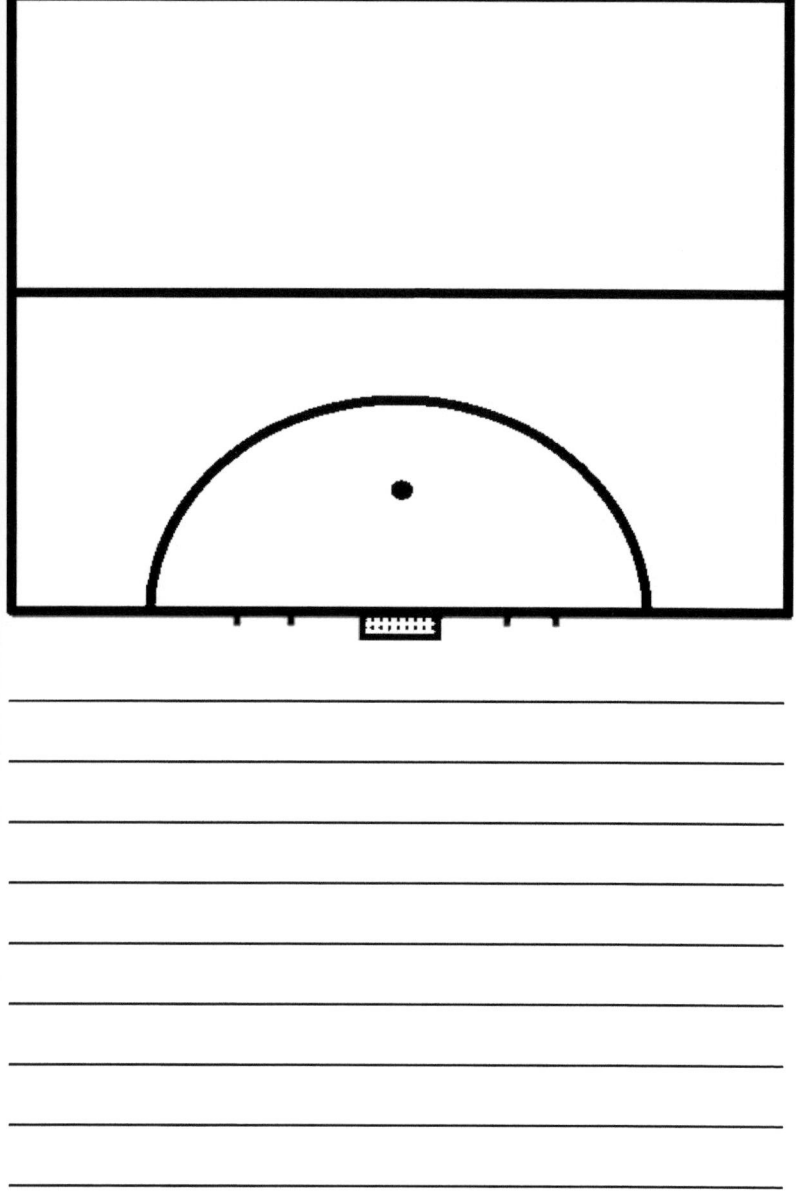

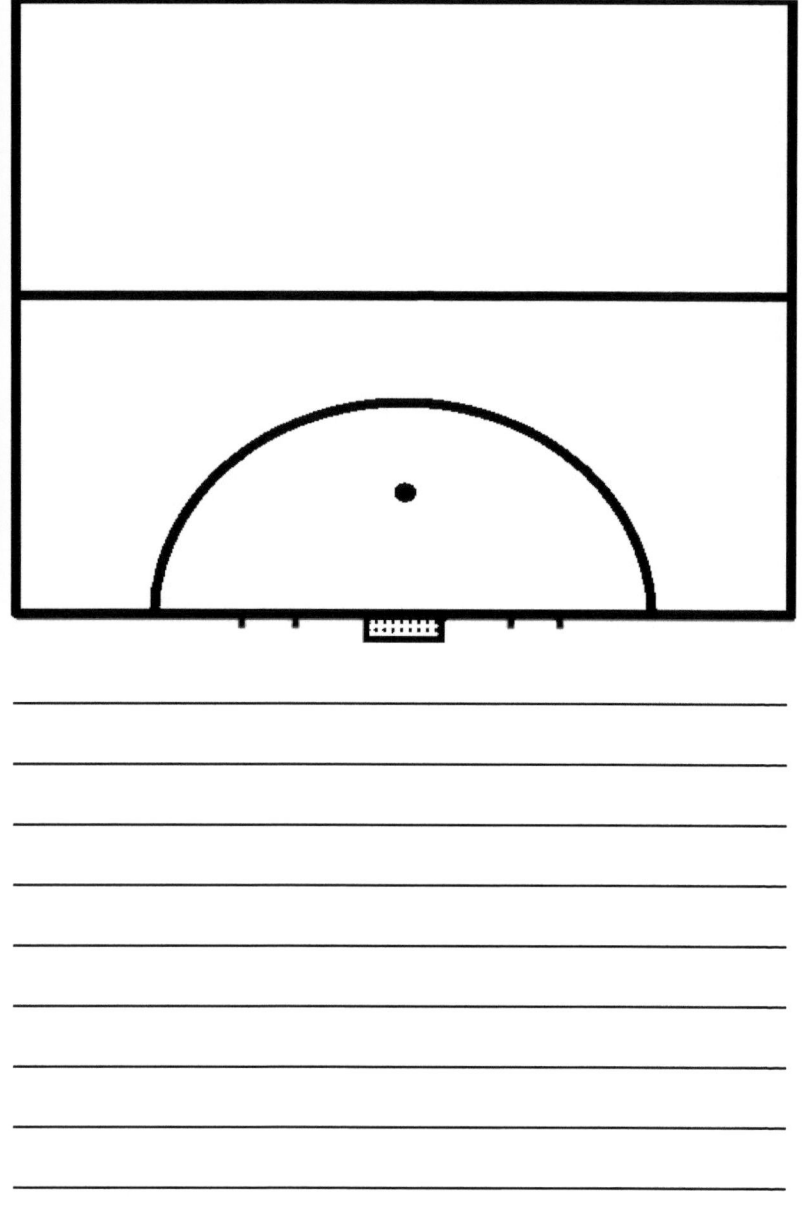

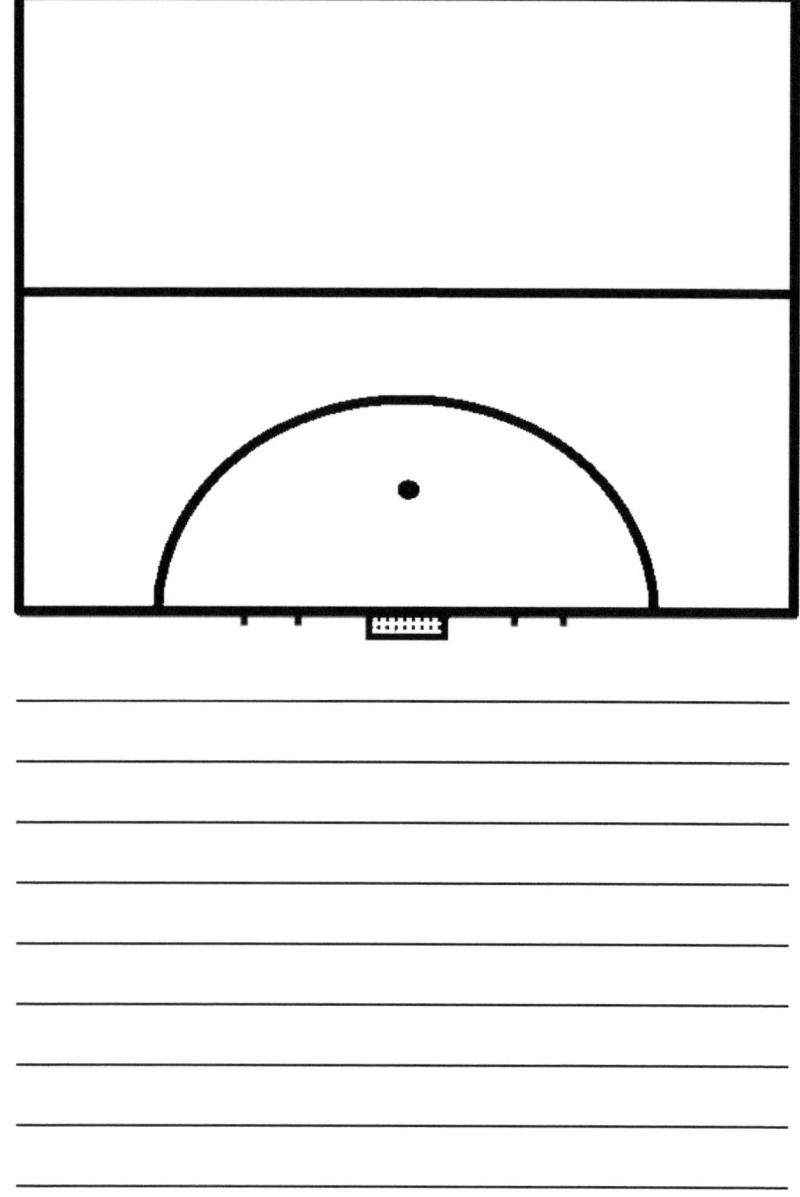

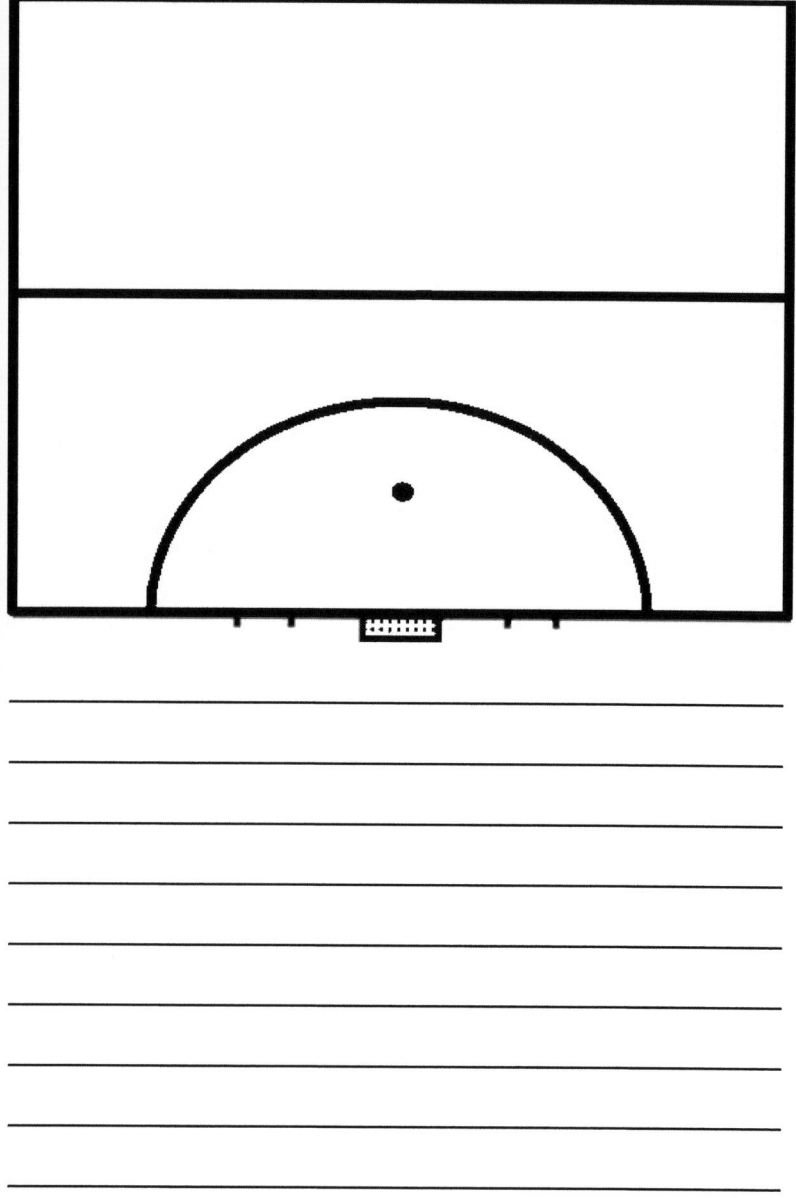

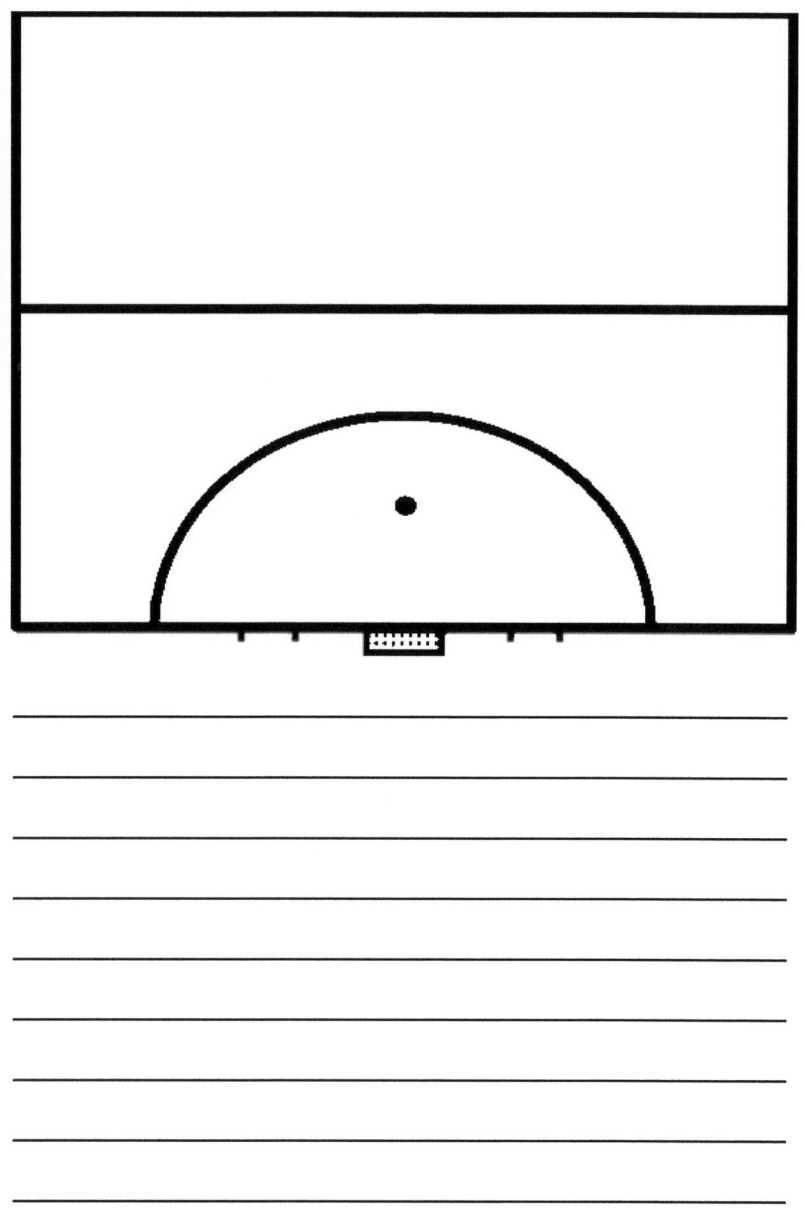

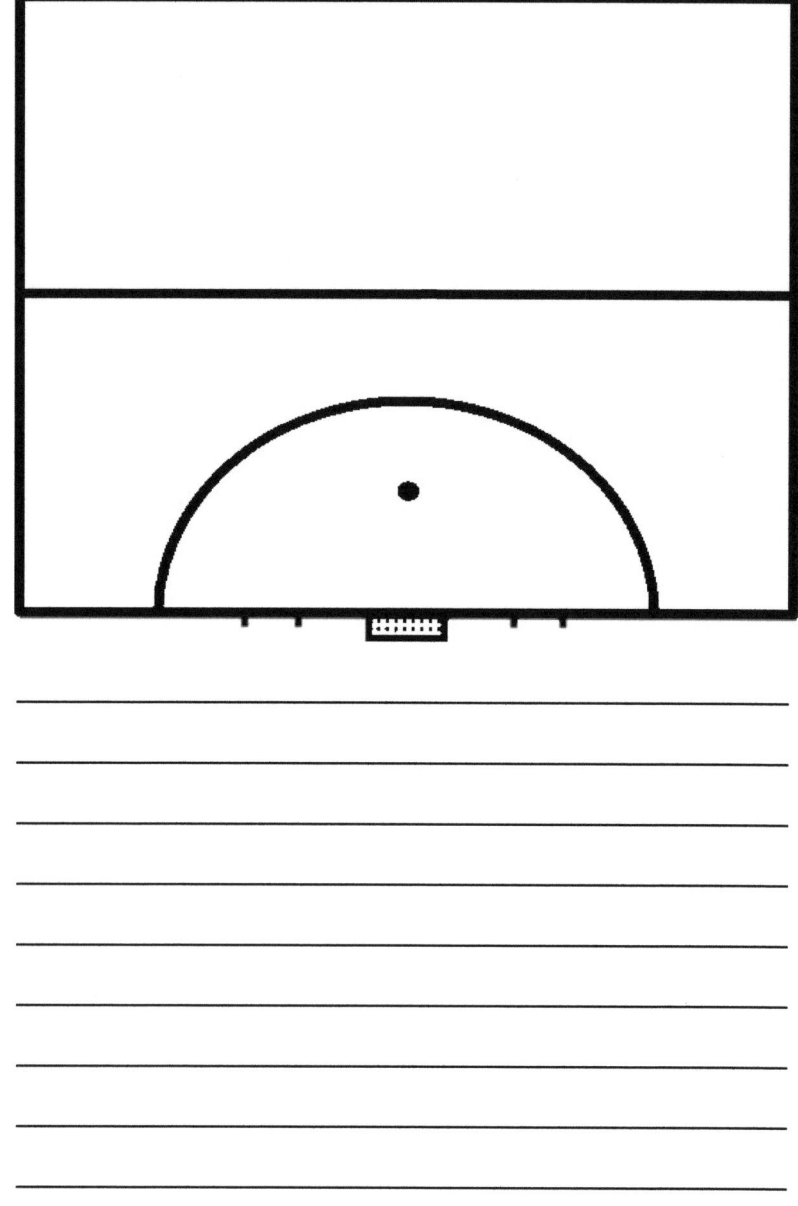

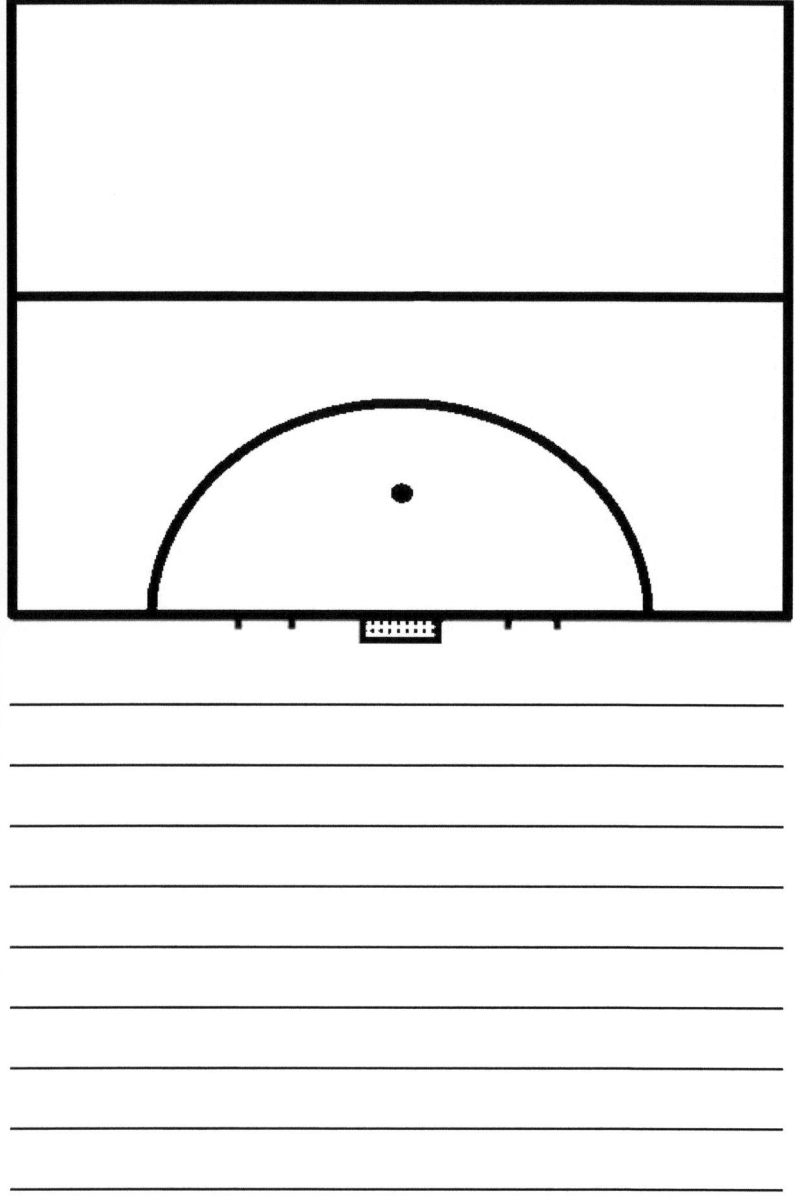

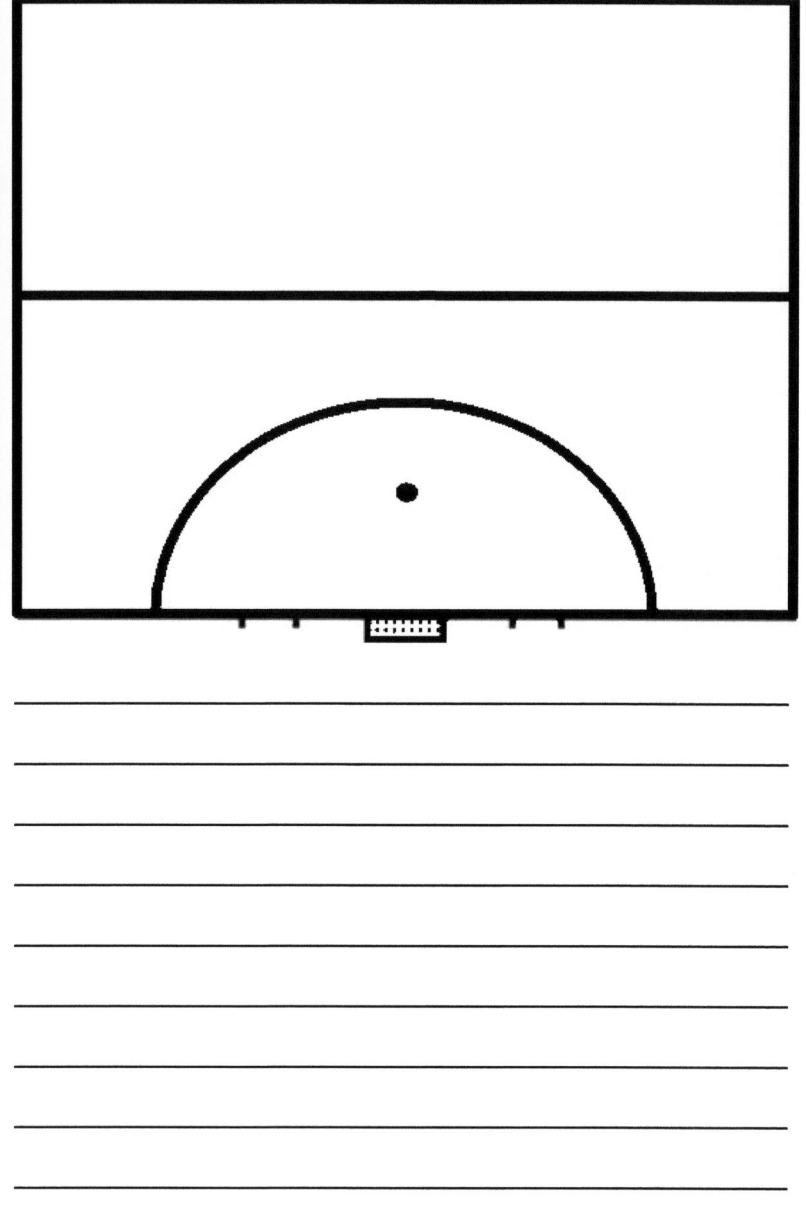

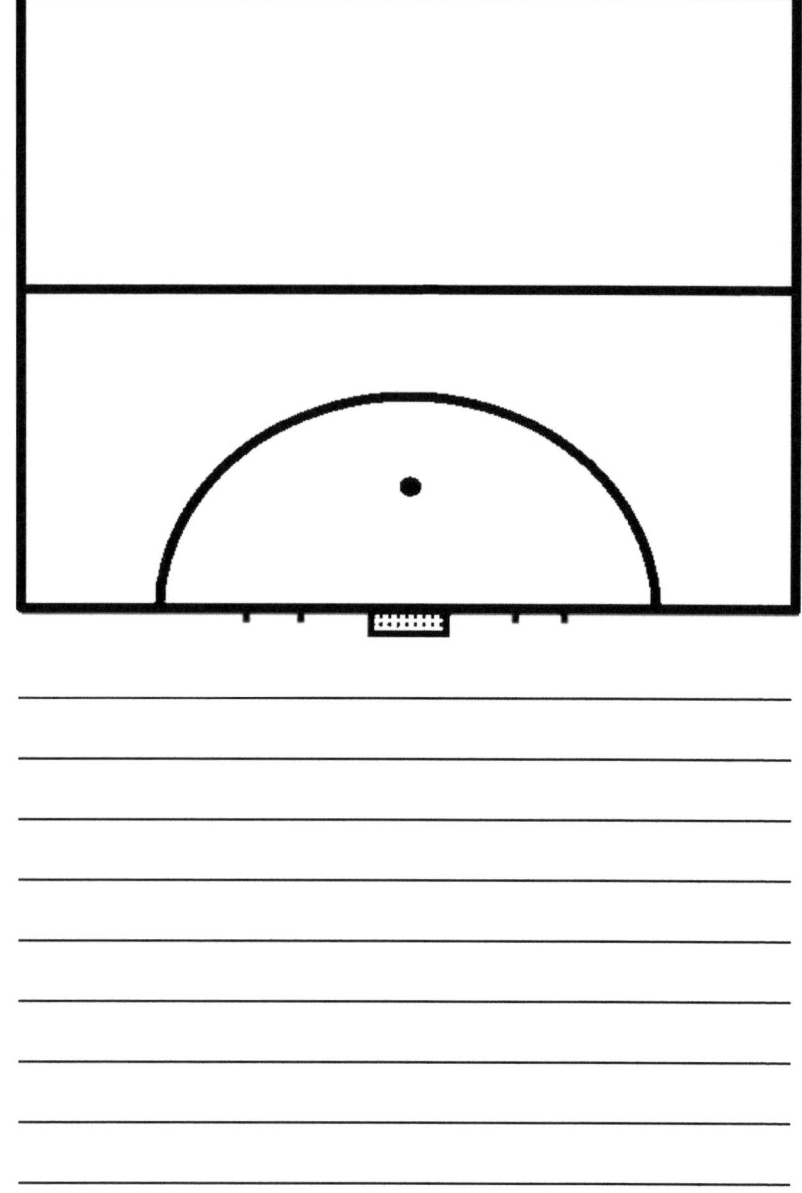

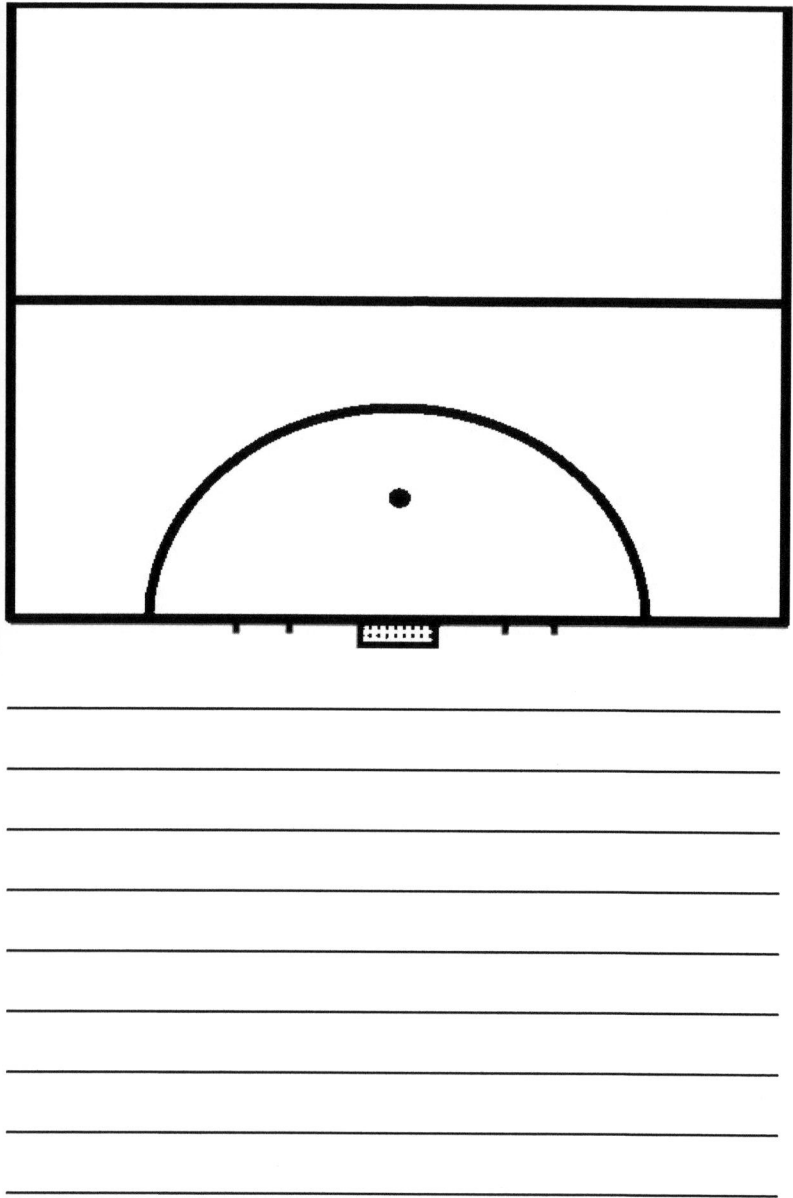

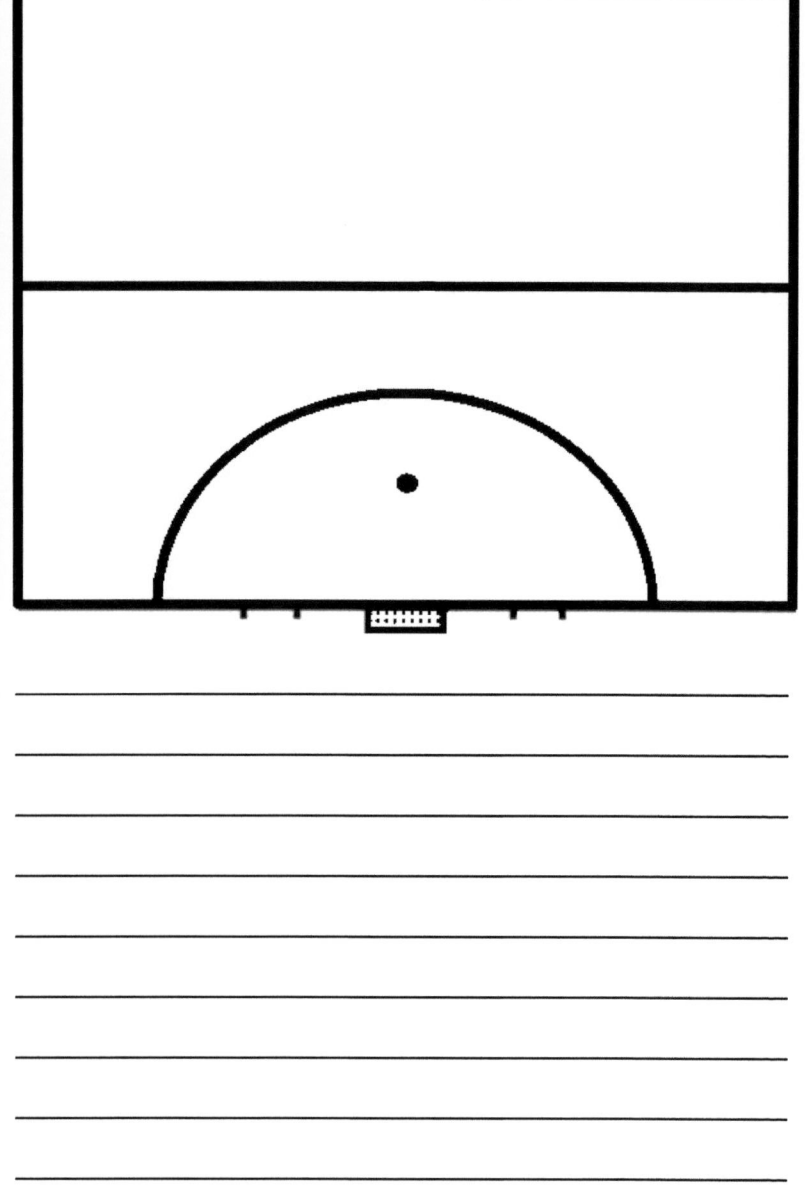

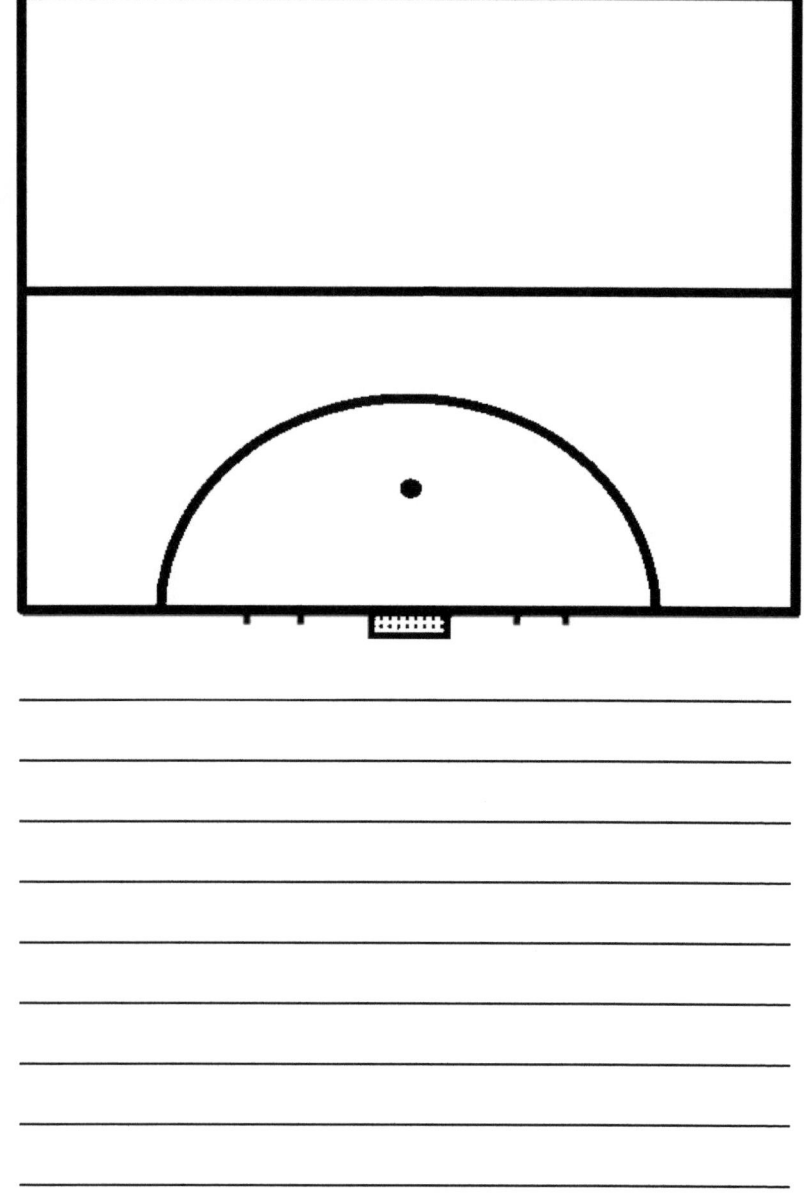

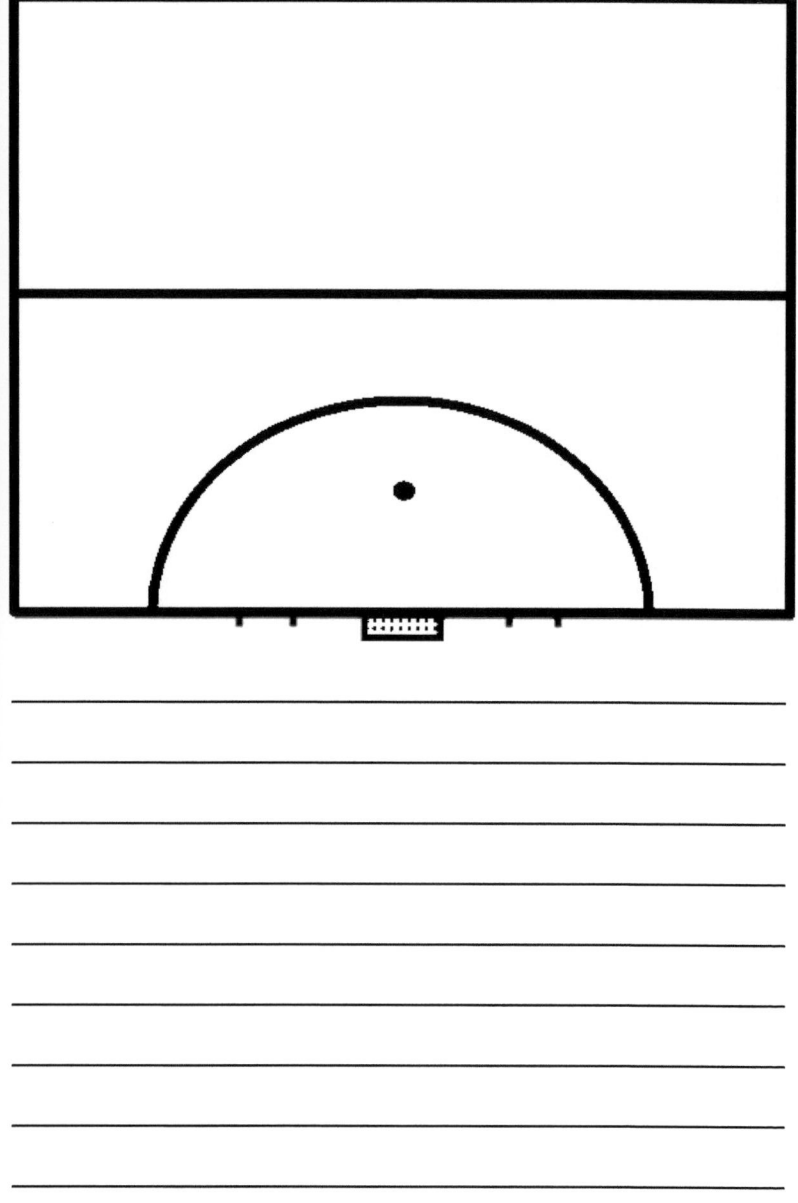

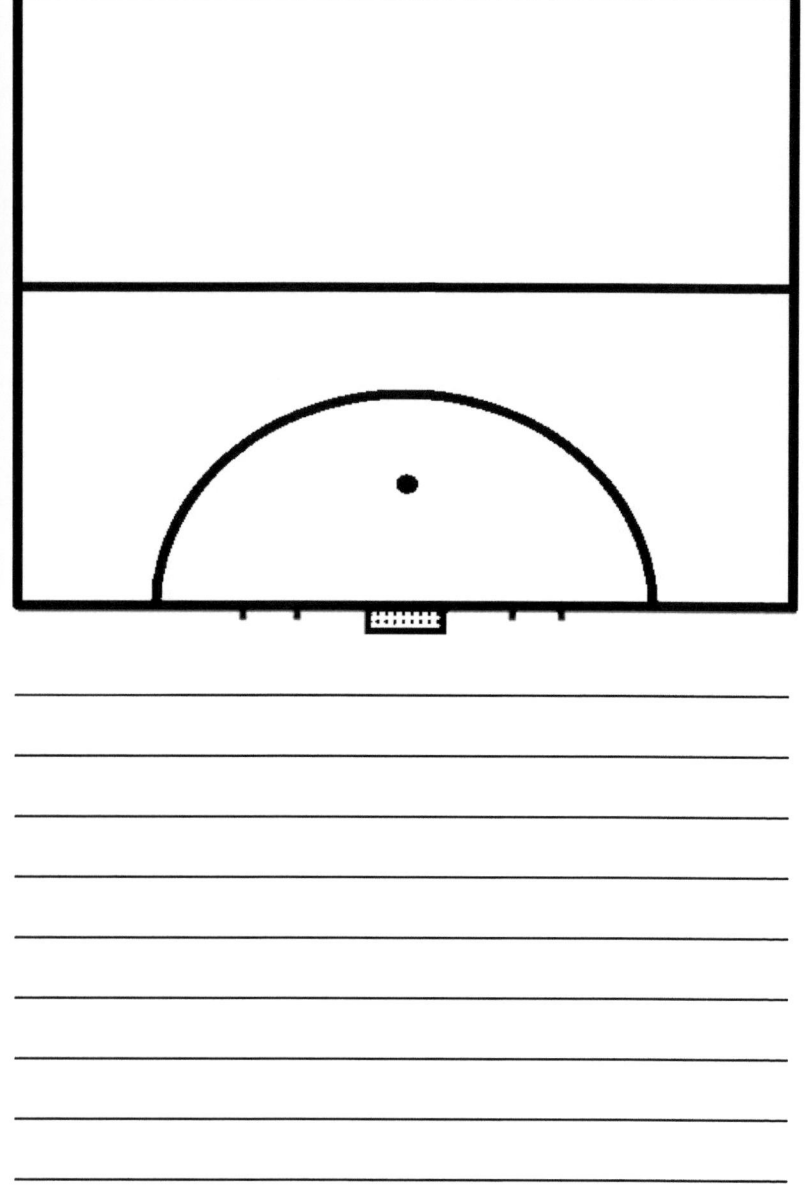

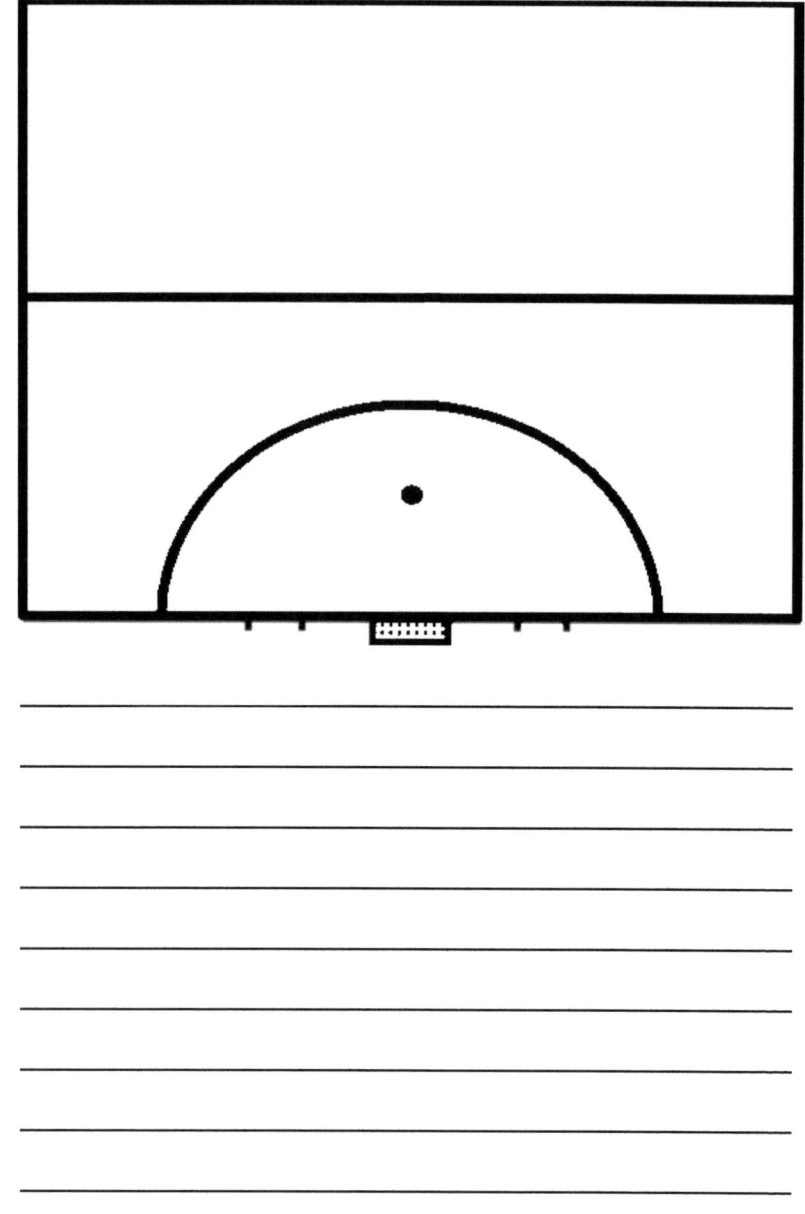

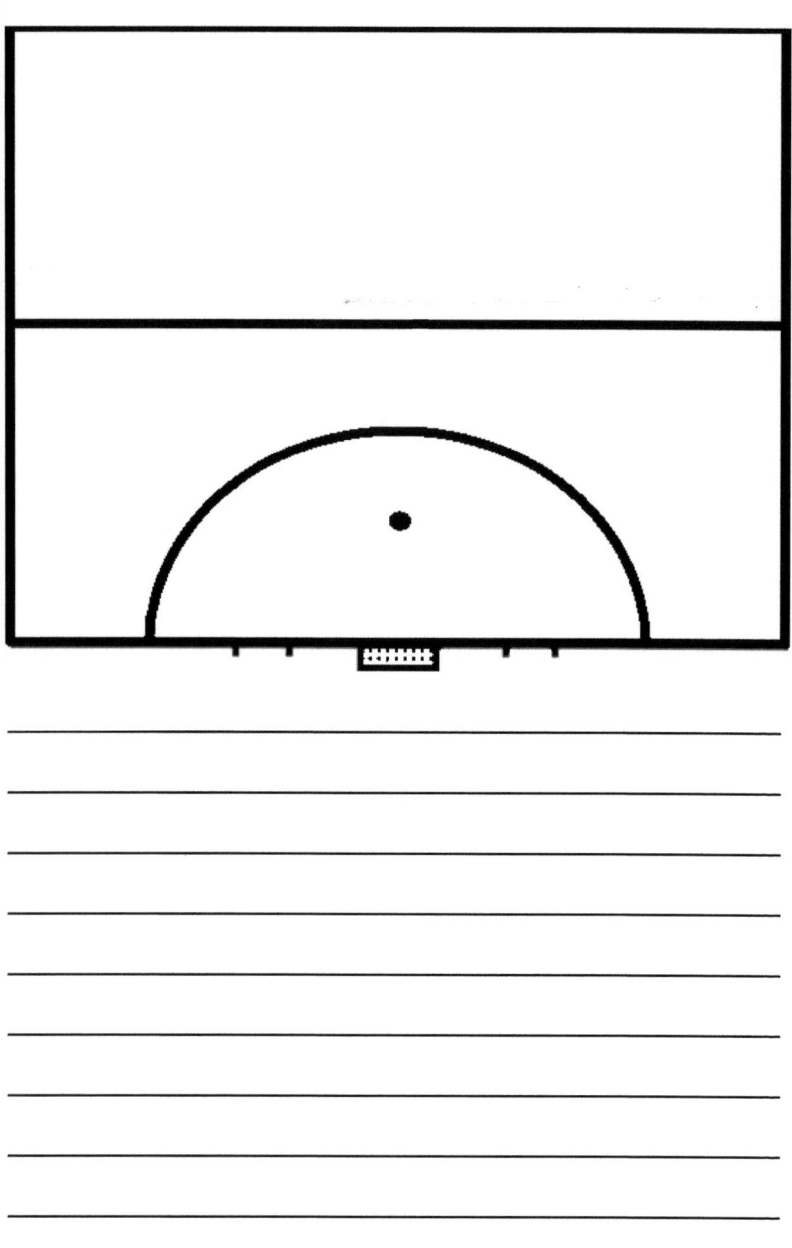

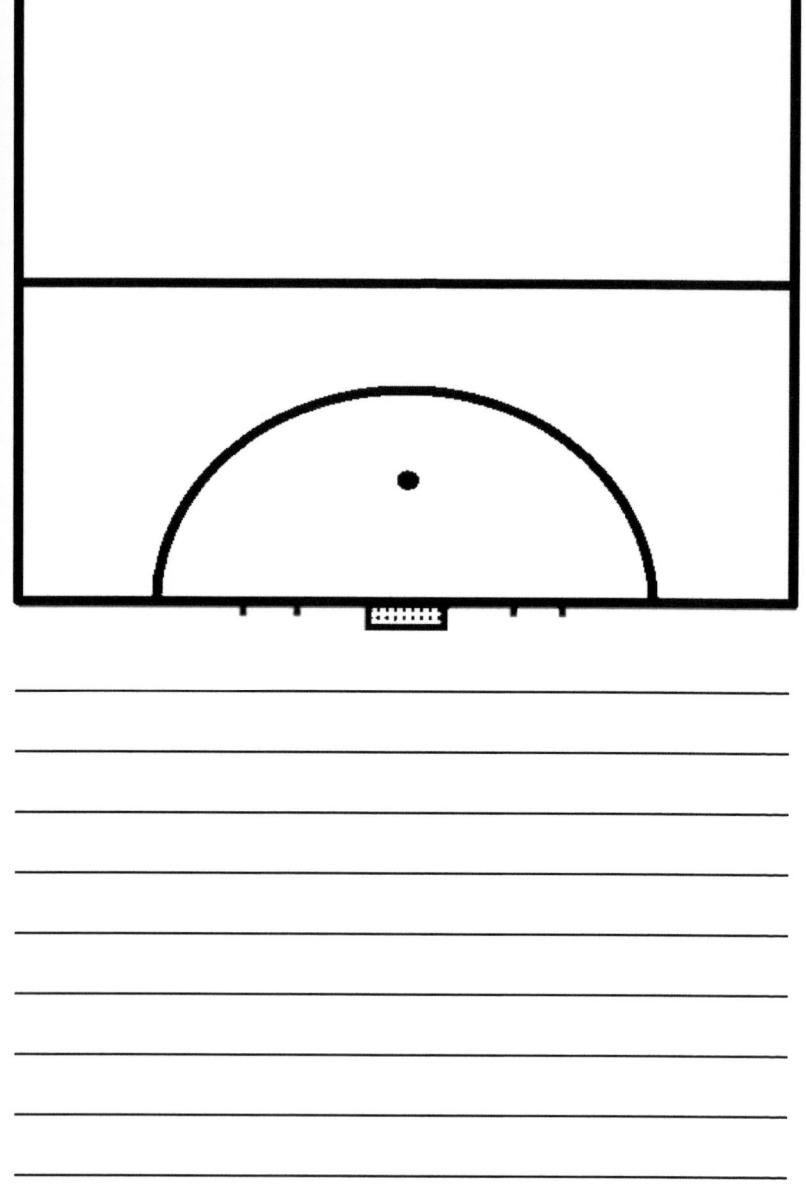

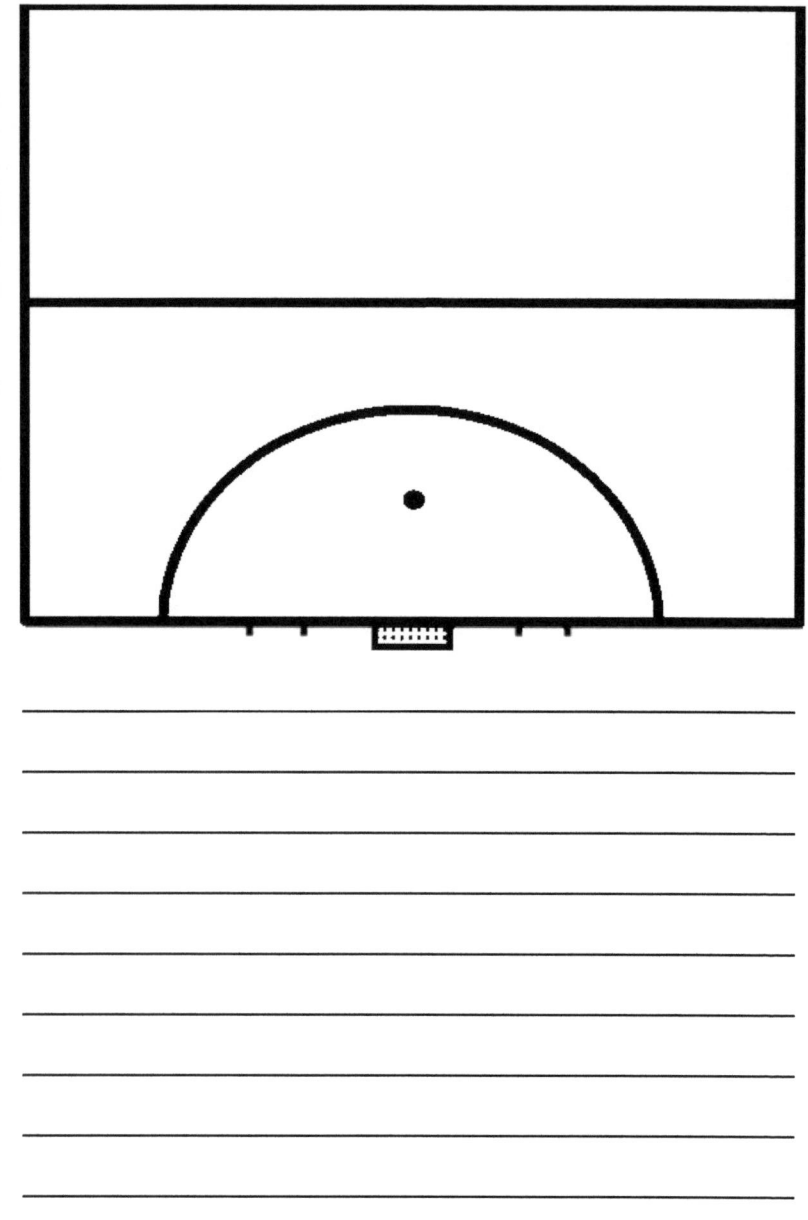

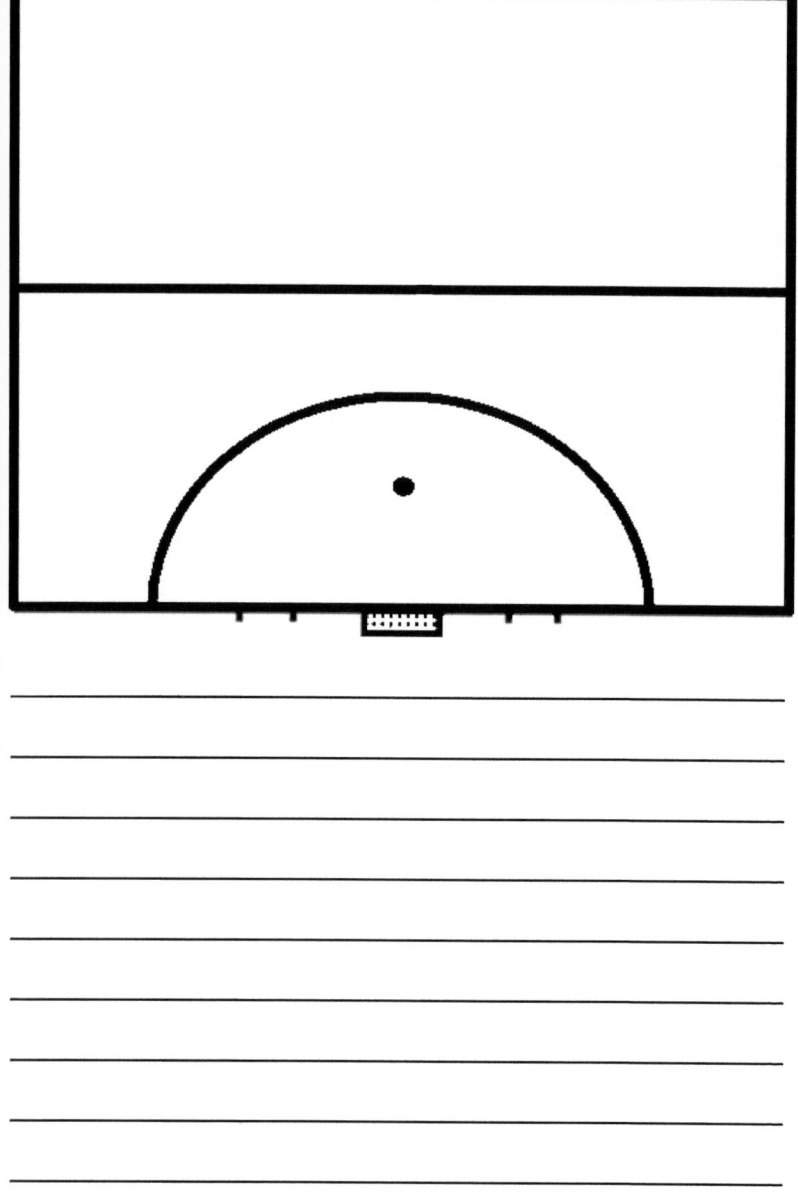

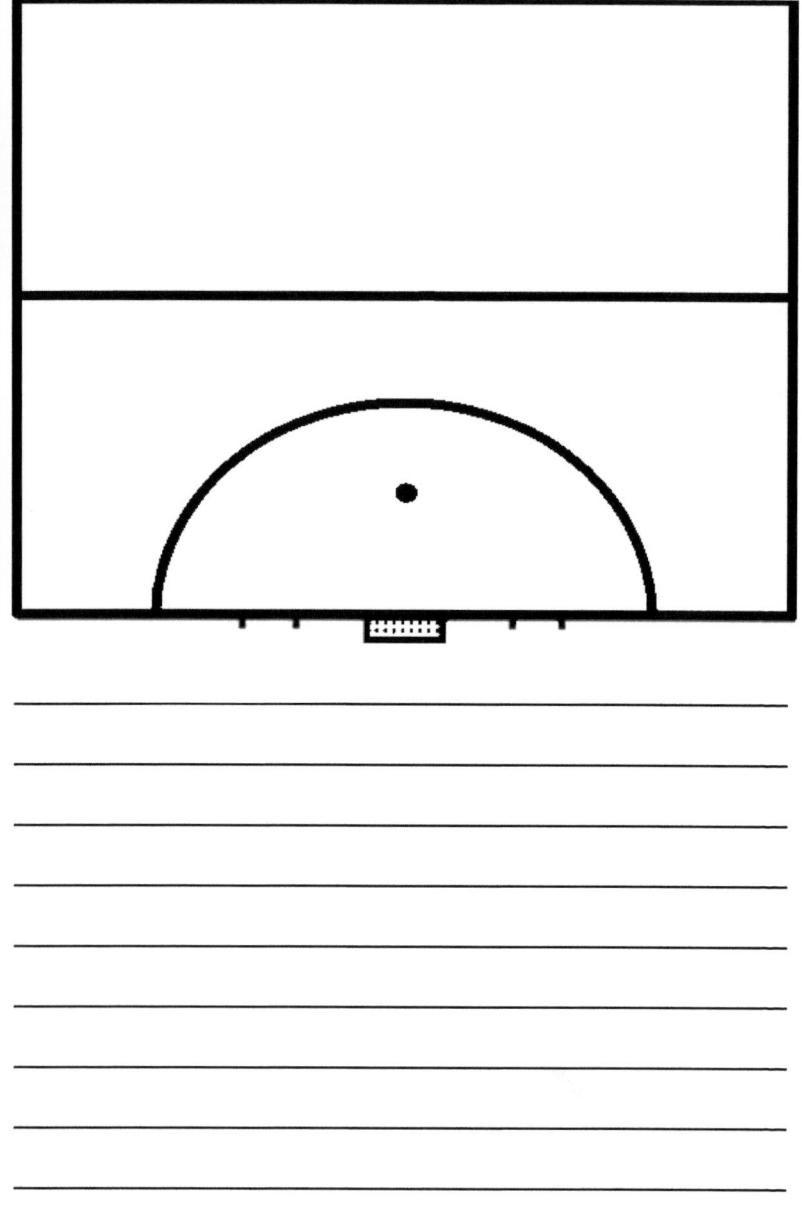

Books of Theo von Taane

book	ISBN / order nr.
Football Tacticboard & Training Workbook	9783734749605
Badminton Tacticboard & Training Workbook	9783734749643
Baseball Tacticboard & Training Workbook	9783734749650
Basketball Tacticboard & Training Workbook	9783734749681
Bowling Tacticboard & Training Workbook	9783734749698
Cricket Tacticboard & Training Workbook	9783734749711
Ice Hockey Tacticboard & Training Workbook	9783734749728
Fencing Tacticboard & Training Workbook	9783734749735
Field Hockey Tacticboard & Training Workbook	9783734749810
Football (Soccer) Tacticboard & Training Workbook	9783734749827
Futsal Tacticboard & Training Workbook	9783734749834
Handball Tacticboard & Training Workbook	9783734749841
Lacrosse Women Tacticboard & Training Workbook	9783734749858
Lacrosse Men Tacticboard & Training Workbook	9783734749865
Netball Tacticboard & Training Workbook	9783734749872
Rugby Tacticboard & Training Workbook	9783734749889
Chess Tacticboard & Training Workbook	9783734749896
Squash Tacticboard & Training Workbook	9783734749902
Tennis Tacticboard & Training Workbook	9783734749919
Table Tennis Tacticboard & Training Workbook	9783734749926
Volleyball Tacticboard & Training Workbook	9783734749933
Water Polo Tacticboard & Training Workbook	9783734749940

Majestic Flowers and Butterflies
- Adult Coloring Book - ISBN: 9783739227085

This coloring book for adults contains 36 beautiful patterns of various flowers. Experience hours full of stress relief, mindful calm, creative expression and fun.

Use crayons, felt-tip pens and colored pencils to give the patterns a personal touch.

Millions of people worldwide have rediscovered the simple relaxation and joy of coloring!

Join this community and find yourself enchanted by the magical passion of inspiring coloring.